ROSH HASHANAH AND YOM KIPPUR

A TRUE BOOK

by

Dana Meachen Rau

Children's Press®

A Division of Scholastic Inc.

New York Toronto London Auckland Sydney
Mexico City New Delhi Hong Kong
Danbury, Connecticut

Kindness to others
is an important part of
the High Holy Days.

Reading Consultant
Nanci Vargus
Primary Multiage Teacher
Decatur Township Schools
Indianapolis, Indiana

The photograph on the cover
shows children eating apples
as part of Rosh Hashanah.
The photograph on the title
page shows a young boy
blowing the shofar.

Library of Congress Cataloging-in-Publication Data

Rau, Dana Meachen, 1971-
    Rosh Hashanah and Yom Kippur / by Dana Meachen Rau.
        p. cm.—(A true book)
    Includes bibliographical references and index.
    ISBN 0-516-22243-0 (lib. bdg.) 0-516-27345-0 (pbk.)
    1. High Holidays—Juvenile literature. [1. Rosh ha-Shanah. 2. Yom Kippur.
3. Holidays.] I. Series.

BM693.H5 R38 2001
296.4'31—dc21   00-060217

Contents

During the High Holy Days, a rabbi leads families and children in prayer at the synagogue.

The Jewish New Year

Early autumn is a very important time of year for Jewish people. During this time, they celebrate the High Holy Days. The High Holy Days are holidays that begin with Rosh Hashanah (rosh ha-SHA-na) and end ten days later with Yom Kippur (yome kee-POOR). Jewish people have celebrated Rosh Hashanah and Yom Kippur for thousands of years.

Every year, Jewish people thank God for creating the world by celebrating Rosh Hashanah. Just as each person is one year older on his or her birthday, the

Just as you have birthdays, Rosh Hashanah is the birthday of the world.

world is one year older on this holy day. Rosh Hashanah means "Head of the Year" in Hebrew. It marks the beginning of a new year and falls on the first two days of the Hebrew month of Tishrei (TISH-ray).

On Rosh Hashanah everyone wishes each other a happy new year. They say the Hebrew words *shanah tovah*, which mean "a good year!" They might send Rosh Hashanah cards to those who live far

At dinner on Rosh Hashanah, families raise their glasses and wish each other *"Shanah tovah!"*

away. Some people buy cards in a store, but some of the best cards are made by hand.

Rosh Hashanah is called a "Day of Remembering." On

this day, Jews remember what they have done since the last Rosh Hashanah. Have they done any good deeds? Are there things that they wish they had done better?

Another name for Rosh Hashanah is "Day of Judgment." It is said that God keeps a book with every person's name in it and keeps track of everything they do. In this way, Jewish people are held responsible for all of their actions.

The Hebrew Calendar

The ancient Hebrews used to look to the seasons to figure out the days, weeks, and months in a year. Then, around 350 C.E., a monthly calendar was created based on the movement of the moon.

In the Hebrew calendar, there are twelve months. Each month has 29 or 30 days. When the days in a Hebrew calendar year are added up, there are a total of 354 days. The calendar we use every day is based on the movement of the sun and is 365 1/4 days long. Because the Hebrew calendar is shorter, about every three years an extra month is added. This month is called Adar (a-DAR) 2.

Months		Holidays
Tishrei (TISH-ray)	(September-October)	Rosh Hashanah, Yom Kippur Sukkot (soo-COAT), Shemini Atzeret (sh-MEE-nee a-TZER-et)/ Simchat Torah (sim-HOT toe-RAH)
Heshvan (HESH-van)	(October-November)	
Kislev (KEES-lev)	(November-December)	Chanukah (ha-noo-KAH)
Tevet (TE-vet)	(December-January)	Fast of Tevet
Shevat (shvat)	(January-February)	Tu B'Shevat (tu B'SHVAT)
Adar (a-DAR)	(February-March)	Purim (POOR-im)
Nisan (ni-SAN)	(March-April)	Passover (*Pesach* [pay-sah]), Holocaust Remembrance Day (*Yom HaShoah*)
Iyar (ee-YAR)	(April-May)	Independence Day (*Yom Ha'atzmaut* [yome HA-atz-ma-OOT]), Jerusalem Day (*Yom Yerushalayim* [yome ye-ROO-sha-LIE-yim])
Sivan (SEE-von)	(May-June)	Shavuot (shav-u-OAT)
Tammuz (tam-MUZ)	(June-July)	Fast of Tammuz
Av	(July-August)	Tisha B'Av, Tu B'Av
Elul (e-LOOL)	(August-September)	

Celebrating Rosh Hashanah

Rosh Hashanah begins when the sun goes down and lasts until the next evening. When the sun goes down, Jewish people go to the synagogue to welcome in the New Year. They attend a service filled with special prayers. During this time, people think about the mistakes they may have made and how they are going to make up for them. They greet each other by saying, "Be inscribed and sealed for a good year!"

The next morning, instead of going to school and work, families go to the synagogue again. During the service, they say prayers and read from the Torah. Everyone waits to hear the blowing of the shofar (show-FAR).

During the morning service, members of the congregation read from the Torah and then blow the shofar.

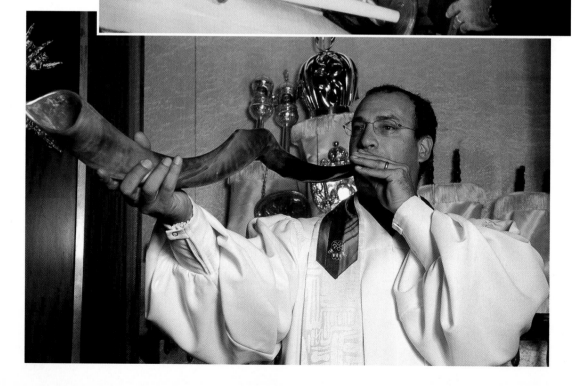

The shofar is a horn, often made out of the horn of a male sheep, a ram. The shofar is hollow, and when it is blown the sound is sharp and loud. Rosh Hashanah is also called "The Day of Sounding the Shofar." The shofar reminds people of stories of the past. It reminds them of the story of a very faithful man named Abraham who sacrificed a ram to God. It also reminds them of when the prophet Moses

called his people together to
obey God. Some say the horn
tells them to wake up and
think about what they can do
to become better people.

The shofar makes four special sounds: *tekiah* (t'kee-AH), the sound of telling people to pay attention; *shevarim* (sh'vah-REEM), the sound of different hopes people have for a good year; *teruah* (t'roo-AH), the sound of calling people together; and *tekiah gedolah* (t'kee-AH ge-DOH-la), the sound of people welcoming the New Year.

When it is time to blow the shofar, everyone stands and

17

recites a prayer. Then someone calls out which notes need to be played. The notes are played in groups of three. The blower plays one very long blast of the *tekiah gedola* at the end.

Some Jews practice a tradition called *tashlich* (TASH-lih) after Rosh Hashanah services in the synagogue. They gather at a nearby stream or river, recite passages from the Torah, and toss bread crumbs into the water. Some Jews even shake out the lint from their pockets.

Families gather near a stream to practice tashlich after services at the synagogue.

This is a way of showing God that they are throwing away the bad things they may have done. The water washes away the mistakes, so they can make a fresh start for the new year.

At Home

In the evening, Jewish people enjoy a holiday meal with family and friends. They light candles and say a blessing to welcome the New Year. They also recite the *sheheheyanu* (sheh-HEH-hee-A-new). This blessing thanks God for life and for allowing them to reach the New Year.

Before dinner, members of the family say blessings for a happy and healthy New Year.

On the dinner table is a plate of apple slices and a bowl of honey. Each family member takes an apple slice and dips it into the honey.

By dipping apples in honey (right), people hope that everyone will be generous and kind to each other during the coming year. Challah (below) is shaped round, like a circle. It reminds people that the year comes around and starts again.

When they eat the apples, they wish that they will have a sweet New Year. They hope that people will be kind to one another and that they will all be happy and healthy. They say, "May the New Year be a sweet one."

Challah (HA-la) bread is also on the table. Challah is usually braided in an oval shape. But for Rosh Hashanah the bread is round. The round shape reminds people that the year comes around and starts again. Challah also might be in the shape of a ladder or of a dove—symbols of prayers being brought up to God. Some people add raisins to the dough to add a sweet taste, or they may dip a piece of it in the honey.

Often, families eat fish. Fish are a symbol of knowledge, because their eyes are always open. They also symbolize having many children because fish lay many eggs. The head of the fish is placed on a special plate. A family member says a prayer about being more like the head of the fish than like the tail. In other words, a person should be more like a leader than a follower.

Thanking God

On Rosh Hashanah, Jewish people thank God for the people who love those who are sad, who take care of those who are sick, who forgive those who make mistakes, and who teach new things to those who need help.

There are many generous activities that people do for others during the year. They read to those who can't read, they help those who can't walk, and they visit those who are sick.

Days of Awe

The ten days leading up to Yom Kippur are called the Days of Awe. During this serious time, people think about the past year and how to best prepare themselves for the new one.

Jews believe that people try to be good. But they also believe that everyone makes

During the Days of Awe, people think about what they have done in the past year and look forward to the new one.

mistakes, even adults. Making a mistake is choosing to do the wrong thing instead of the right thing. When someone makes a mistake, he or she misses the chance to do something right.

What if someone forgot to invite a new student to a party?

27

She might not have known at the time that she was making a mistake. What if someone else ate a cookie even though his mother had asked him to wait until after dinner? He knew he was making a mistake when he did it. In both examples, they missed their chance to do the right thing.

To be close to God again, people need to make up for their mistakes. Doing *teshuvah* (te-SHOOV-ah) is how they can make things right again. But

We can make up for our mistakes in many ways, such as making our bed or helping someone with the groceries.

how does this work? First, the person has to admit he or she made a mistake. Next, he or she makes up for it.

One of the most important parts of the ten days is saying sorry to God and to the people who have been hurt. Learning from past mistakes and changing what has happened are important so that the same mistakes will not happen again.

Another important part of the holiday is charity, or giving to others. In Eastern Europe, it was a custom before Rosh Hashanah for someone to walk from house to house with a sack. If a family had a lot of money, they would drop some into the sack. If a family didn't have enough, they would take some out. Today, people might do charity work at a shelter or soup kitchen. They might donate food to needy families. Some give money to help the poor. Others find a way to keep God's world beautiful, such as cleaning up a local park.

The Eve of Yom Kippur

The night before Yom Kippur is a time to prepare for the one of the holiest days in the Jewish year. Some wear their best clothes. People light holiday candles and say prayers for those who have died. They also light another candle called a memorial or *yahrzeit* (YAR-tzite)

נר שעוה

A yahrzeit candle
helps people
remember
someone they love.

candle. The yahrzeit candle
burns for the entire holiday. It
helps people remember those
who are no longer alive.

Before sunset, families sit
down for a large meal. Once
the sun goes down, the
adults will not eat or drink

until sundown the next night. This is called fasting.

It is hard not to eat or drink anything for a whole day. Fasting reminds people that they are human. They make mistakes, unlike God who is perfect. It also allows people the time to pray. Children are not expected to fast, but they might try to give up some type of food for the day, such as snacks or other treats.

After the large meal, families go to the synagogue. A special prayer called *Kol Nidre*

(coal NEE-dray) is chanted three times. It is an ancient prayer with a powerful melody. The prayer talks about the importance of the words people speak. It also talks about new beginnings.

At the Synagogue

Yom Kippur means the "Day of Atonement" in Hebrew. Atonement means being forgiven for sins. Yom Kippur is not spent at home. Families spend the whole day at the synagogue. The congregation prays together for the sins of the community. Some people hit their chests with their fists as they mention each sin. It is a way of showing how sorry they are. Several times during the service they sing a special prayer called *Avinu Malkenu* (a-VEE-new mal-KAY-new). This prayer asks God to forgive and treat everyone kindly.

Another important part of the service is when the congregation reads from the prayer book about what life was like in Jerusalem about two thousand

This engraving (top) shows the Temple of Jerusalem. The Western wall of the temple, also called the Wailing Wall, still stands today. A man blows the shofar for a crowd at the Wailing Wall (bottom).

years ago. The Temple of Jerusalem was a very beautiful and special place where Jewish people worshipped God. It was the center of Jewish life. The High Priest would enter the Temple on Yom Kippur and ask forgiveness from God for the sins of all the Jewish people. When he came out, he sent a goat who "held" all of their sins out into the wilderness. There was much singing and dancing.

In the Book of Jonah, a great fish swallows Jonah. After three days and nights, God answers Jonah's prayers and sets him free.

During the afternoon service, the Book of Jonah is read. From it, people learn that God answers prayers, and God forgives His people when they pray to him, no matter how sinful they are.

Another service in the after-noon called *Yizkor* (YIZ-ker) is said to honor people who have died. It is about the importance of family and learning from loved ones. At the end of the last service just after sunset, the shofar is blown only once. The sound wishes everyone a good new year and marks the end of Yom Kippur. The service lasts until people can see at least three stars in the night sky.

After the services, families go home and eat a large meal to break the fast. They may invite friends to join them. They eat many traditional foods, such as challah and matzah ball soup, or other tasty foods, such as bagels, lox, and cheese. This is a happy time when everyone enjoys eating together.

The High Holy Days are a special time for Jewish

families to gather and start the New Year free from the mistakes of the year before. It is a time to feel close to God and family and to apologize to others who have been hurt. It is a time to make up for sins and to try to make better choices. The most important thing to remember is that God loves His people. He knows they make mistakes and sees the good in everyone.

To Find Out More

Here are more places to learn about Rosh Hashanah, Yom Kippur, and other holidays:

 **Books**

Chaikin, Miriam. **Menorahs, Mezuzas, and Other Jewish Symbols.** Clarion Books, 1990.

Groner, Judyth S. and Madeline Wikler. **All About Rosh Hashanah.** Kar-Ben Books, 1997.

Groner, Judyth S. and Madeline Wikler. **All About Yom Kippur.** Kar-Ben Books, 1997.

Stoppleman, Monica. **Jewish.** Children's Press, 1996.

Wood, Angela. **Judaism.** Thomson Learning, 1995.

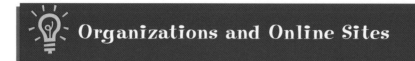

Organizations and Online Sites

Books for Jewish Children and Teens

http://www.geocities.com/ CollegePark/6174/ jewish-children.htm

Books of all types are listed at this site for readers who want to find out more about Jewish traditions, history, and holidays.

Jewish Family and Life

56 Kearney Road
Suite B
Needham, MA 02494
http://www.jewishfamily.com

This online magazine is for the whole family! It includes articles, recipes, art projects, and information about upcoming holidays.

Torah Tots

http://www.torahtots.com

This online site is dedicated to children. It includes information about holidays and other fun activities.

Yom Tov

http://www.torah.org/ learning/yomtov/

At this site, take a "class" on the Jewish holidays that are celebrated throughout the year.

Important Words

ancient from very early in history

atonement being forgiven for sins

C.E. stands for Common Era

challah a braided bread made with eggs

forgiven when someone accepts your apology

Hebrew having to do with Jews or the Jewish religion; a language spoken by many Jews

rabbi a Jewish leader

sacrifice to give up something for someone else

sin something one has done wrong against God or another person

symbol something that stands for something else

synagogue a place where Jewish people meet to pray and worship

Torah a sacred Jewish book

Index

Meet the Author

Ever since Dana Meachen Rau can remember, she has loved to write. A graduate of Trinity College in Hartford, Connecticut, Dana works as a children's book editor and has authored more than forty books for children, including biographies, nonfiction, early readers, and historical fiction. She has also won writing awards for her short stories.

When Dana is not writing, she is spending time with her husband, Chris, and son, Charlie, in Farmington, Connecticut.